1

treble clef

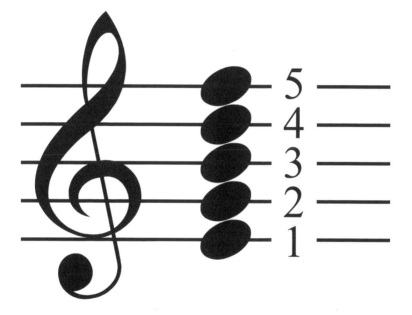

1. E

2. G

3. B

4. D

5. F

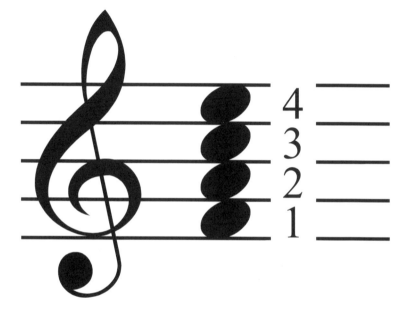

1. F
2. A
3. C
4. E

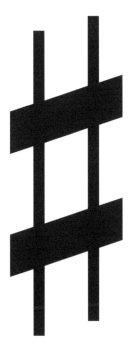

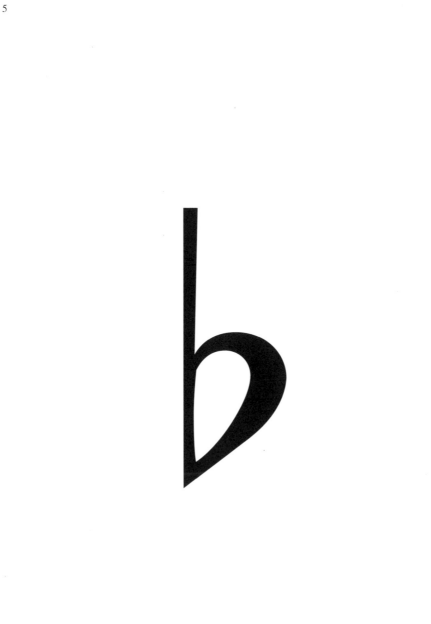

flat

whole
note

half
note

quarter note

eighth
note

dotted
quarter
note

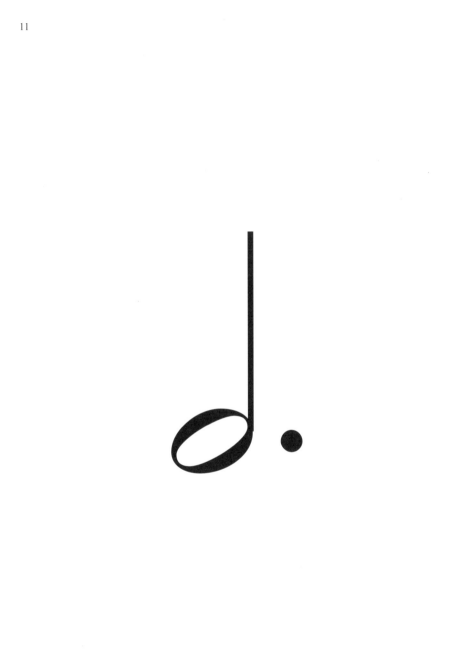

dotted
half
note

triplets

whole
rest

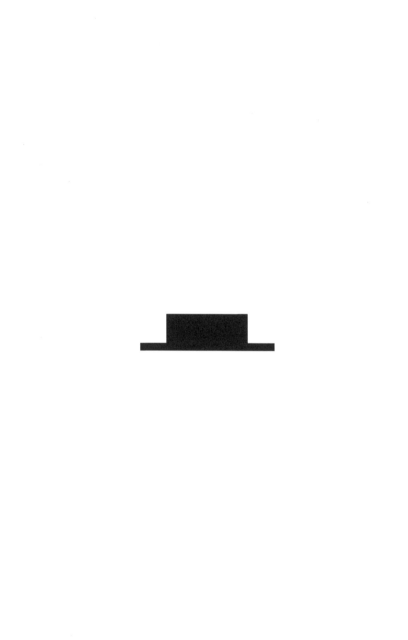

half
rest

quarter rest

eighth
rest

$$\frac{4}{4} \text{ or } \mathbf{C}$$

$\frac{4}{4}$ time

four beats per
measure, quarter
note gets one beat

$\frac{3}{4}$ time

three beats per measure, quarter note gets one beat

68

$\frac{6}{8}$ time

six beats per measure, eighth note gets one beat

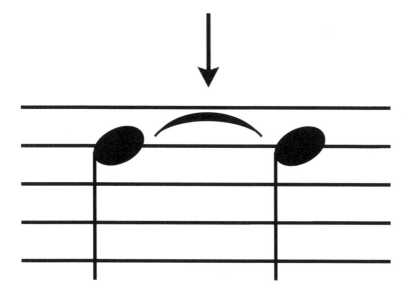

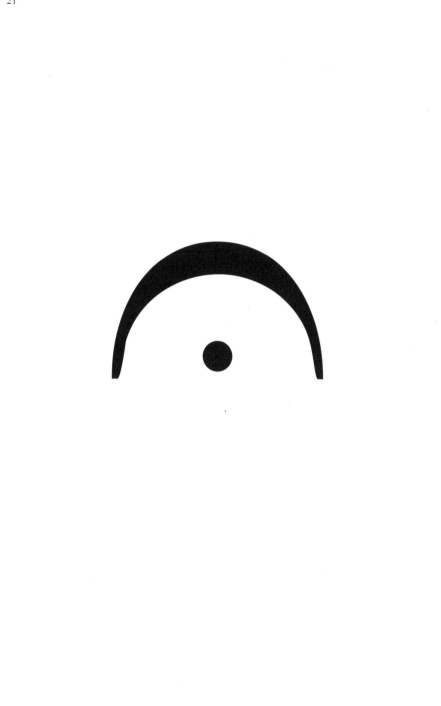

fermata

downstroke

tremolo

Tempo

rate of
speed

Dynamics

how loud or
soft to play

Interval

the distance
between
two pitches

repeat
signs

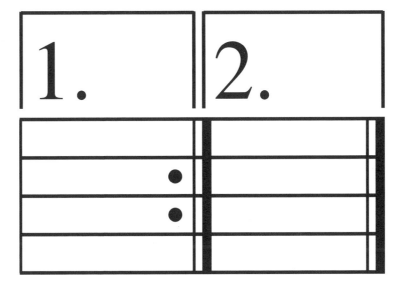

D.C. al Coda

Return to the
beginning
(capo) and play
until the first
coda sign ⊕
then skip to the
next coda sign

D.S. al Coda

Return to the
segno sign 𝄋
and play until
the first coda
sign ⊕ then
skip to the next
coda sign

D.S. al Fine

Return to the segno sign 𝄋 and play to the end (fine)

33

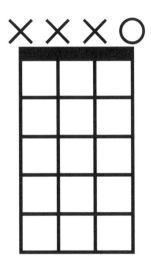

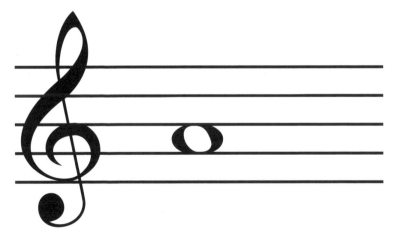

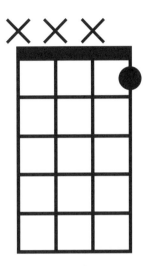

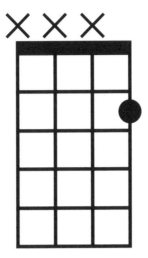

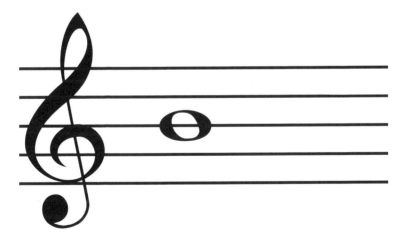

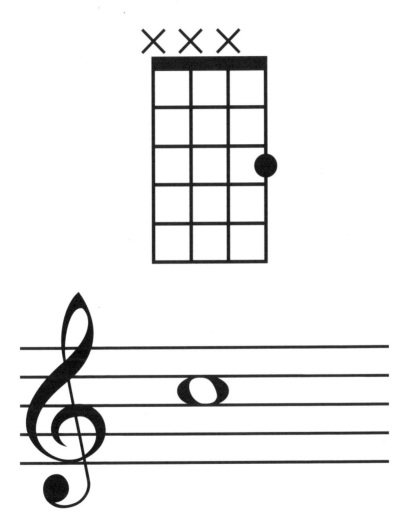

C

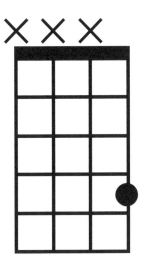

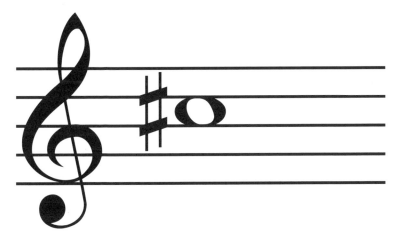

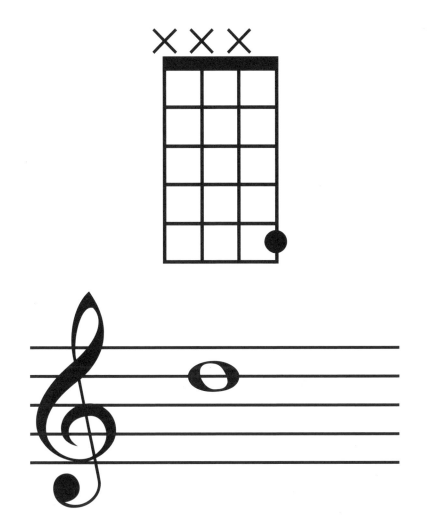

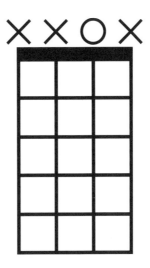

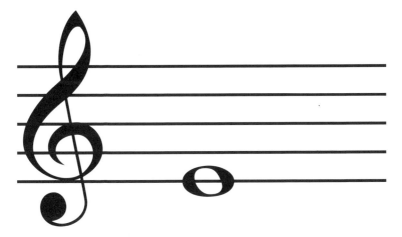

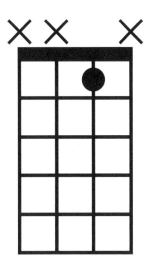

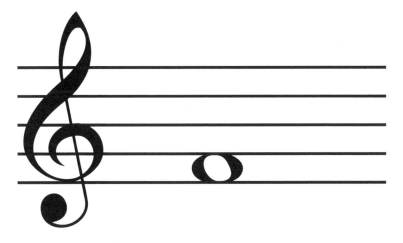

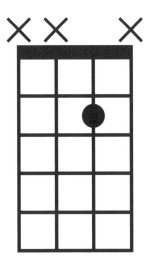

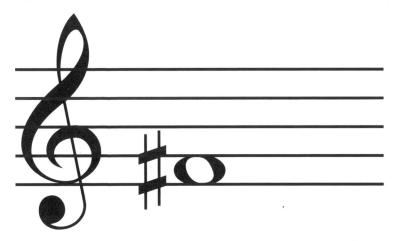

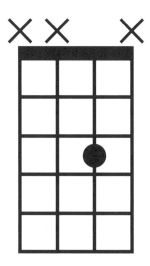

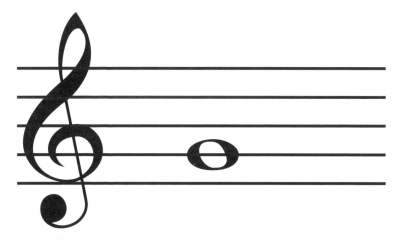

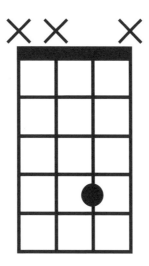

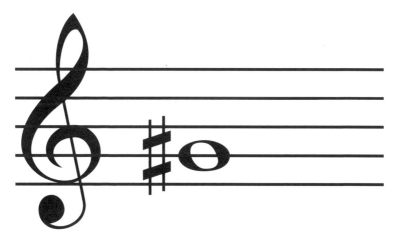

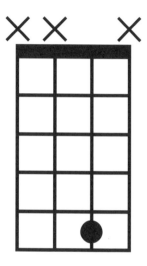

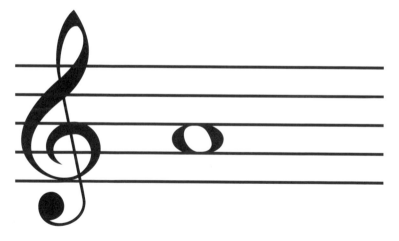

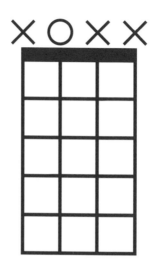

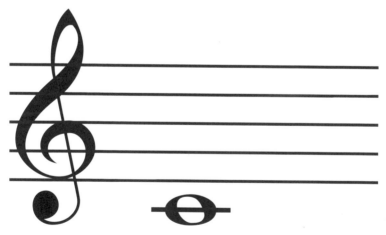

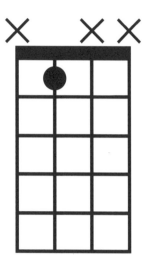

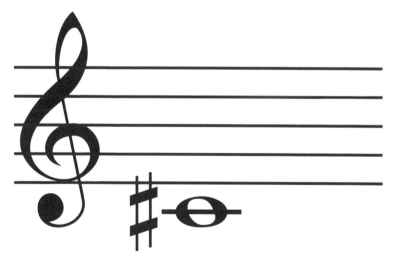

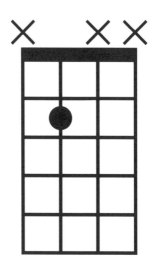

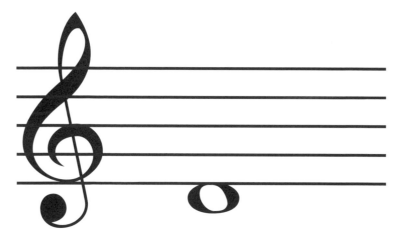

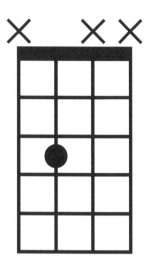

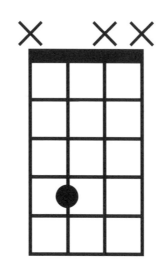

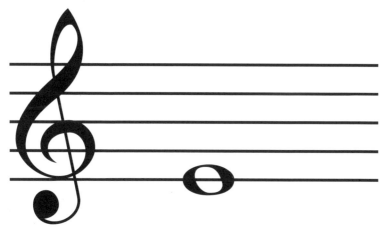

E

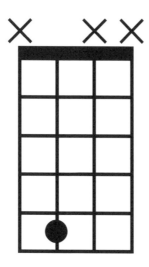

F

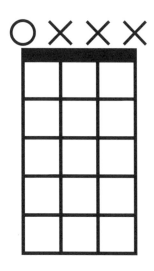

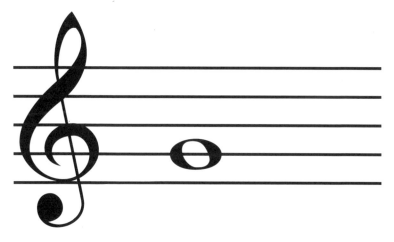

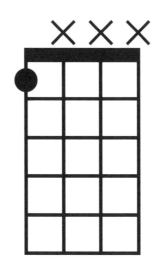

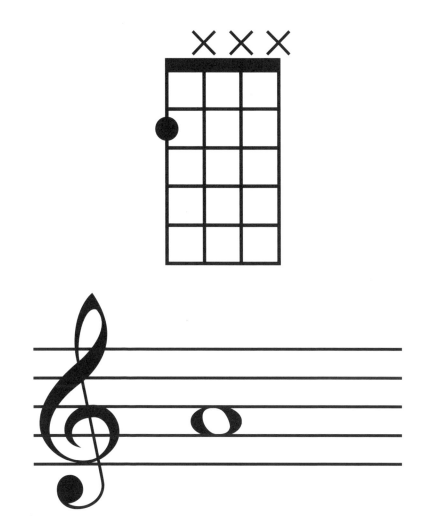

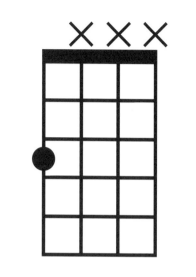

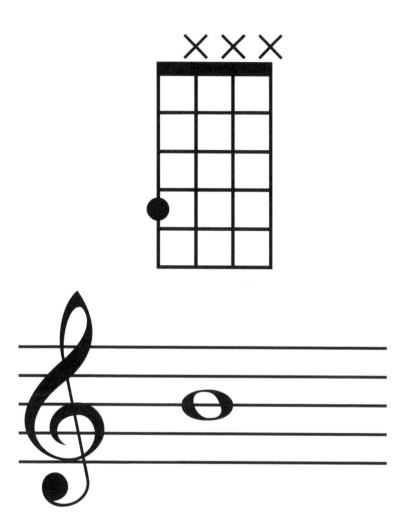

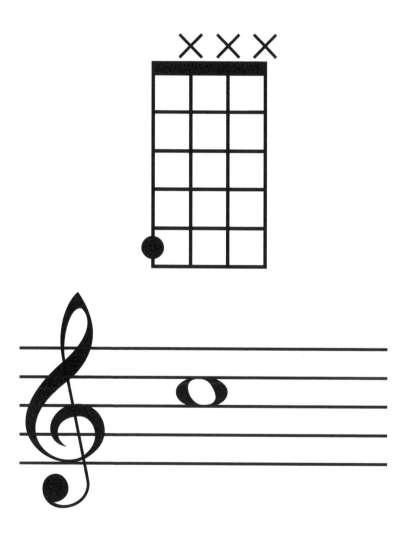

C

C major
A minor

G major
E minor

D major

B minor

A major
F♯ minor

E major
C♯ minor

F major
D minor

Bb major
G minor

Eb major
C minor

A♭ major
F minor

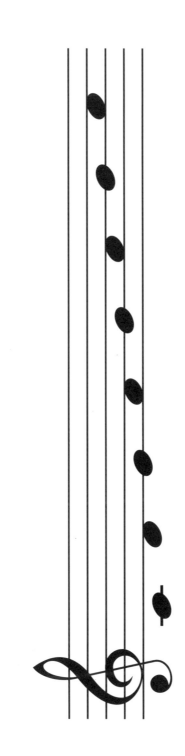

major scale

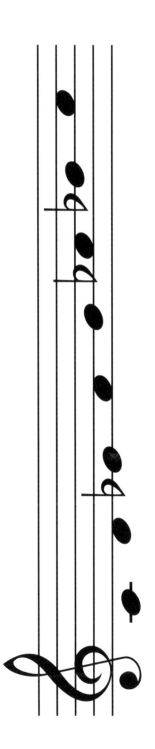

natural minor scale

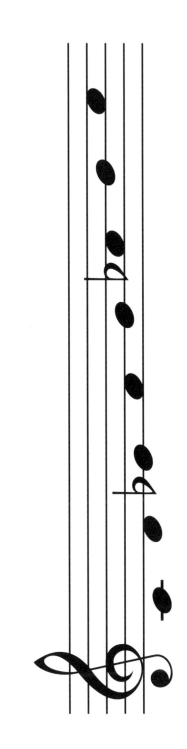

harmonic minor scale

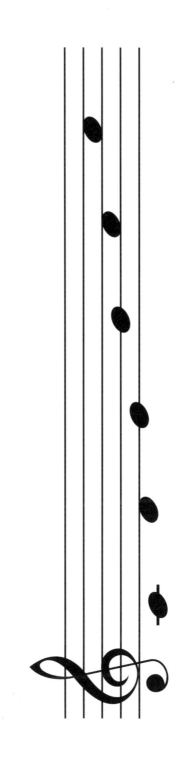

major pentatonic scale

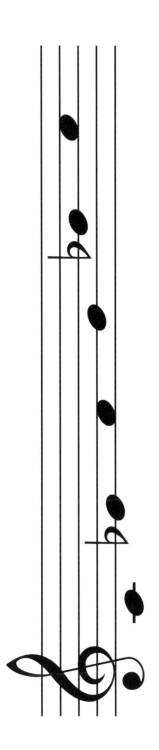

minor pentatonic scale

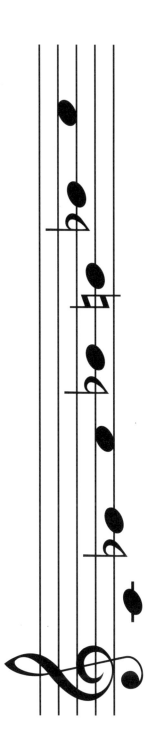

blues scale

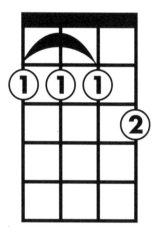

D7

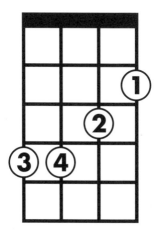

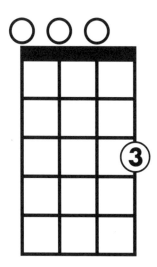

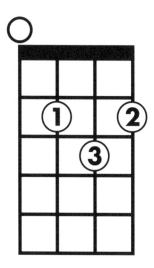

G

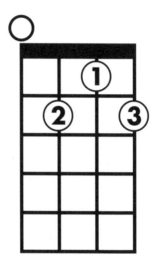

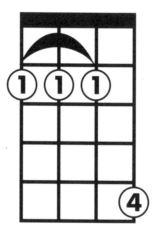

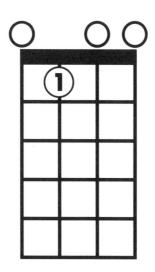

A7

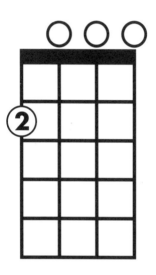

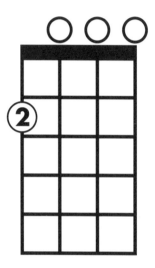

Am

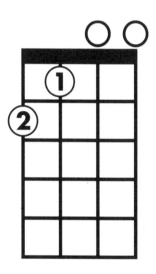

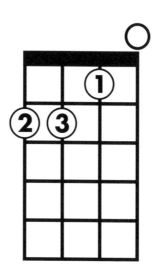

Dm

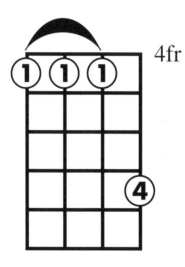

4fr

E

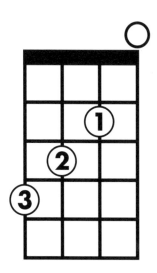

B7

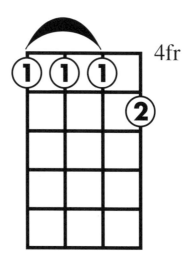

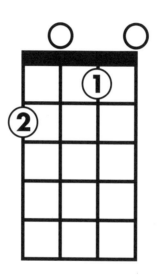

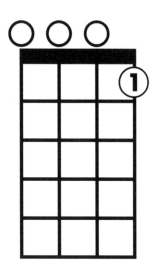

C7

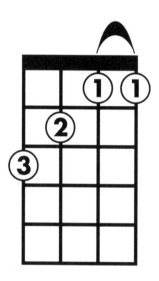

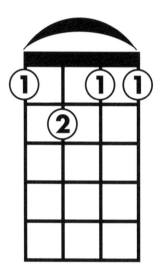

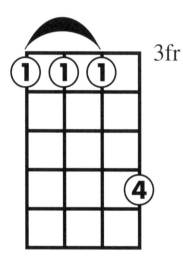

3fr

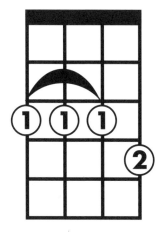

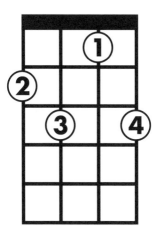

F7

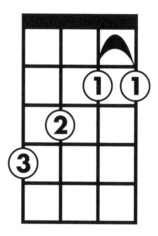

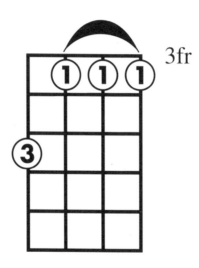

3fr

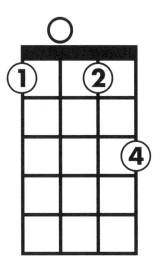

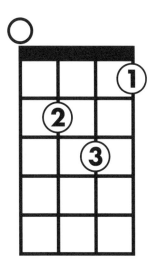

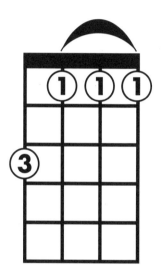

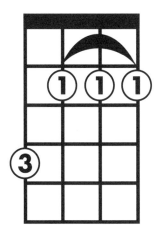

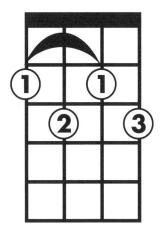

Adim7

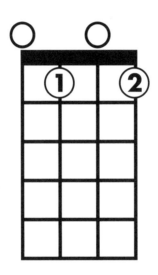

C#dim7